People watching and brain searching

Kristian J Williams
People watching and brain searching

Published by BooxAi
ISBN: 978-965-578-541-8

People watching and brain searching

KRISSY WILLIAMS

She has gone away

I lean into the prenotion that you'll return even though there are no signs of it.

There are days I convince myself to ignore the fantasy so I clean what is left of you behind.

Goodwill was scheduled for a house call on the first of the month so I started the process of separating clothes from hangers.

It was easier to begin with the winter apparel.

I folded a crew neck sweater made for your 13th birthday.

Your aunt hand-stitched it in 3 days and you attempted to unravel it in one.

The Burberry coat from New Year harbored the smell of your collection of perfumes you'd find from magazine catalogs.

You'd cut out the scent strip and stick it into a drawer of shirts until you saved up enough to buy the real thing.

I managed to collect half of the closet space before exiting, leaving piles of clothes laying on the carpet.

It's too difficult to see the remnants of you.

You wouldn't want to see me like this: my flushed face blistering against the bathroom floor.

The sharp coldness of the tile broke the fog I was in and I remembered to cry.

In a month's time, a mouse family inhabited the fabrics of your sweaters and coats, their small heads popping in and out of gnawed holes whenever I took a look inside your room.

The neighbor, Cassie, lent me her unsolicited advice and some cardboard boxes for your old clothes.

When I arrived to her house, tucked away in the trees, she was standing in the doorway, thin and frail like a moth with paper wings hovering near her porch light.

She flashed a knowing smile at me, her smiley piercing glinting off her gums.

Her dreads flowed over her shoulders and down her back.

I didn't want to go to her house but I had to.

Going to the store meant the guarantee that I would be greeted by an employee's animatronic smile to empty large boxes thrown aimlessly in the back aisles.

Going to Cassie's meant that there was a possibility she'd come up empty-handed and I could at least say that I tried to forget you today.

Cassie has a way of prying information out of me, some of which I didn't realize I remembered.

She did the same with you.

I wonder what you told her about me.

I'd watch the two of you from the window, passing a cigarette and secrets to one another.

A sly smile in my direction.

A whisper of laughter.

She was ten years your senior but that didn't stop the two of you from giggling like schoolgirls in a hallway.

Cassie knows things that haven't been unraveled to me yet.

Things I'm not sure I want to know

She's 32 with creases and worry lines as if she's seen things not worth mentioning.

I assume this is why she's unfazed when I tell her everything.

Night murmurs

The heater is too hot
warm chest nearly sweat
sticky
chapped lips and yawn glistened eyes
turn to look at me
make sure i'm tucked away
and unassuming
watch me belly breathe
slide your toes on the carpet
ask questions to the wall about how you will
remember me
will
you
collect jars of my hair strands from the tub
wipe my toothpaste residue on an old t-shirt to have for
safekeeping
hold my drool-stained pillows
and complain about the hair grease on them
make a rosary of my baby teeth

eat the earth from the bottom of my shoes
for now, remember me as i am
savor sweet silences when i sleep
i am not your souvenir
i am here

I think it was the summer of 2018

But how can you say that i'm beautiful if you haven't seen
me in all of my forms
when I was hunched over in the bathroom
cracked tooth in the sink
salt water in my eyes
sticky blood on my tongue
prying at the throbbing gap of gums
if you'd asked I would tell you I slipped face-first in hot
concrete
let the sidewalk sizzle my hands until I was aware of my
surroundings
I have a purple and blue badge on my forehead to show
for it
the nurses stared at me with concerned steady eyes
one of them pulled me to the side, cold gripping hands on
my arms
like a mother trying to cough the truth out of her child
she examined the pain in my eyes, the corruption in my

smile, the fleeting hints of truth behind my scars on my
arms and legs
I wallowed in her sympathy until she let go
I heard her whispers come from behind the door, breathy
and trembling
another nurse came in to grab swabs from a cabinet but his
demeanor showed that he came to look at me, staring like I
was an animal at the zoo, head between the bars of
my cage
then I was bandaged like a mummy
got a central incisor implant on a Tuesday
played a game to see how close and far my tongue could
get to my fake tooth
but I was told no touching
I sit near the window most days watching the street
drag my finger around the coffee table's bowl of candy
wonder if tall blue badged uniforms will walk up to my
porch
wonder if the nurse thought of me and my badge and told
them to ask me if I was a girl scout
would they walk through my halls to find my certificate of
honor
stare at the empty walls and find no one but my shadows
in every corner
I'd eat an oreo while they ask questions about who has
floated in and out of the doorway
and I'd laugh because who checks on someone who is
forgotten
but you did

I cannot function but it's okay

I face backwards, head first in a fetal position to process it all, as I was instructed to do in the womb

I always believed that I didn't process the aspects of socialization well for many reasons

When i was smaller, my brain told me that my eyes were a television camera and I had to capture someone or I would get the gnawing feeling in the back of my brain that something bad would happen like a wet lollipop twirled into my hair or wake up with no toes. My mother later berated me for staring. I now do the opposite where I can't look anyone in the eye when I'm speaking.

I consumed parks and rec one summer. I told everyone I absolutely loved it. My mom watched me watch the show in confusion because I would sit there, stone-faced episode after episode without smiling or laughing. She didn't understand how I enjoyed something so much without physically responding. In my head, I thought it was hilarious so once again, I didn't understand what she meant. I see it more clearly now.

I ran orbits around my mother's monologues when she believed her drink was poisoned. She said she knew someone in the family had a life insurance policy taken out on her that one of us would get when she died. I miss who she used to be. I would put flowers in her hair if she would let me.

For me

I am supposed to take RX#182390 every day once a day.
I went off of it for six months.
An old friend came to town to live with my mom for a
while and I'd point at the pharmacy near the strip mall
and go, "That's where I used to get my meds," as if she
needed a landmark for my depression.
At the same pharmacy, she picked up her prescription,
constantly mentioning how it was her first-time taking
meds for any mental health problem and I'd nod thinking
about the last time I remembered to take mine.
Probably five days ago but it's fine.
She took hers with cheap beer we bought from a grocery
store (and then she wondered why the pills didn't work,
which is so ?? Are u dumb).
The lady at the cash register eyed us with mascara-
smeared eyes but didn't ID us.
No one ever IDs me here.
It's weird.
I can't tell if I look 20 now or if people just don't care.

My friend said I look older than her but then again if we
were able to purchase child tickets for the train back to
New York then what's the truth?
The guy who glances at everyone's tickets didn't say a
word.
Maybe he didn't care either.
A bus driver called me a little girl a few weeks ago but I
was wearing a short skirt and no makeup and my voice
was higher-pitched because I was maneuvering between
generalized anxiety and a fear that he would kick me off
the bus because I didn't pay.
Did I have my meds that day?

I didn't

But I have them now and I just saw my psych doctor a few
days ago.

He brings in students in training every time we're on a
Zoom call.
"Do you mind? I have some students here and they're
going to ask you some questions."
Well it's 9 am and I'm tired enough to lie.
It's always about the symptoms.
The dry mouth, the restlessness at night, the changes in
behavior *because last time you were talking about mood
swings, and if it's gotten worse I really think we should look into
that, and are you sure you're sleeping? You look tired. I refilled
the prescription for your sleeping medication and Andrew here is
going to ask you about your day-to-day to see how it affects your
daily activities. Do you mind talking to Andrew? And the pills
can only relieve so much of your anxiety. You have to take on*

I didn't take my meds today.

I saw that the pill bottle fall to the floor and I told myself I would pick it up and take one earlier because I didn't want to take them at night.

I do enough overthinking I don't need pills to aid that.

So I'll take them tomorrow if I remember to.

Or not.

For her

My friends and I took the F train on that Saturday in
September.
I don't fit in much with them but they're good company.
I think you'd like them because they have the same sense
of humor as you,
Laughing over things I'd crack a small smile at.
I felt restless with them.
I could insert myself into the conversation a few times.
But they'd dive deeper into topics I didn't know enough
about.
I could stare out the window at the black walls of the
tunnel.
but I'd probably start dissociating when I needed to be
present.
I just didn't want to look at my phone.
A month prior I debated on whether I'd call you this
Saturday.
I imagined ringing your phone and praying it would go to
voicemail because

I haven't heard your voice in months.
Should I leave a voicemail for you or hope that seeing my
missed call shows my intentions?

There's an announcement of the next stop and my
roommate grabs my arm to pull me off the train.
She likes to loop her arm around mine to chain us
together.
She's wearing a perfume I helped her pick out at the mall
that smells like
an afternoon at an orange grove.
I rub my thumb over the fleece on her sweater.
It's warm.
We enter another train and it's packed with people.
She unlinks our arms and I find a spot at the opposite end
of the train to sit down at.
A man with a purple-collared chihuahua squeezes in next
to me.
His dog is in a carrier bag and I smile when her small head
peeks out to look at me.
If you were here, you'd ask me to ask him if you could
pet her.
You've always liked animals.
I memorized the names of all five of your dogs and what
treats they like.
If things were different this Saturday, I'd show up at your
house as a surprise.
And see your stampede of animals playfully lunge at me
in the doorway.
And you'd apologize like you always did,
giving me an extra kiss to make up for the struggle I'd
have later to get all of the dog furs off of my clothes.

Then I'd settle in your living room,
A gift in hand,
watching you sit beside me with a look of anticipation.

My roommate shouts something to me in between the
rumble of the train tracks.
I can't hear her so she says she'll text it to me.
The chihuahua looks at me drooling and tilting her head to
the side.
As if she senses the dread I feel.
It's an open invitation to scroll over old text messages.
And see in real-time how our innocence slipped away.
I pretend to not see my roommate's question, giving
attention to the black windows instead.

The Letter

Dear Delilah,

Last month, I remembered finding you in my kitchen in the middle of the night propped up on a stool, feet dangling and kicking. You peeled oranges with your chipped fingernails still containing polish you meant to scrub off but never would. I remember watching the way you chewed. It was in the same manner as you did as a child, large hungry bites chewed slowly with wide eyes. Your fingers were soaked from squeezing each slice. You laughed at the mess you made with a mouthful of oranges in the back of your throat. Then out of nowhere, you spotted me at the doorway and gave me the most ridiculous grin.

For a while, I thought the reason I kept replaying this in my head was because I missed you. I missed seeing you wrapped up in a blanket on the sofa, the way you annoyingly talked during movies and stood in front of the screen when I was not paying attention, and how you hummed softly as you walked barefoot through the hallways.

However, I realized this morning that I held that thought of you because it felt familiar. It sparked a memory of us. It came in small flashes so I could be missing some parts but I'm writing down everything I remember.

During the winter we went to Florida. Mom said she didn't like seeing palm trees when Christmas was around the corner because it didn't feel right. You cried mascara tears and sunk your nails into the fake leather of the car in protest of spending the holidays away from your friends. I rolled down my window to grab the air. I liked how different it felt from the wind at home.

Dad wanted us to visit his parents while we were on winter break. He told us that they asked about us all the time. We hadn't seen them since our Pull-Up days so we didn't care.

When we arrived, we gave them obligatory hugs that smelled like fresh laundry. Mom and Dad shared baby photos and clinks of wine glasses while we explored. We found green tea leaves in the fridge, played with glass figurines on the coffee tables, and squeezed into a dirty crawl space. Grandpa pulled me out right when I thought I saw a dead rat inside.

Grandma shooed us to the back door so we could relieve our recklessness outside in the orange grove. With a shaky hand, she pointed out a nearby tree. Large golden oranges hung from their branches. Dad lifted us on his shoulders to pick however many we wanted. Before he put me down, I twisted his curls around my grubby finger and pulled them gently to watch them spring back into place. Grandpa retrieved a hand-woven basket from indoors to help us collect oranges.

As Mom mentioned the pies she could make with

them, a stiff iguana dropped into her glass of wine. She shrieked, chucking the glass to the ground. Red shards bled through blades of grass. Stifled laughter escaped from our grandparents' hidden smiles. Dad turned around with you on his shoulders. He explained that iguanas often slept in the trees and become immobile when it's cold, causing them to fall. For the rest of our stay, she kept her wine indoors.

"First entry completed." Lynn scanned the page again then flicked her eyes up at me. I could tell from the way her right hand was perched on the page that she was about to ask me for specifics. "Thank you for making me a copy. Also, I wanted to ask if you were nervous about doing this assignment."

Lynn, my therapist, was lanky and awkward. The temperature spike this morning made her look longer than usual. Her legs jutted out of her plaid tweed skirt, her bare arms overextended across my paper. Fall in Seattle is flip-flops and ice-chewing season and she was dressed accordingly. She crouched over her desk like a toddler hunched over their coloring book, crayons grasped in their sweaty fist. If it wasn't for the specks of gray in her roots, she could pass as a woman in her thirties. Her baby face showed no signs of aging. I wished to look like her when I was older; fresh-faced and soft.

Her mini fan hummed quietly in the corner of the room pushing stiff air around us. It wasn't too hot in her office but it was bearable enough to not need the windows open.

I chewed on the inside of my lip before answering, "I

was nervous about what my brain would come up with while writing. I expected to have this really emotional breakthrough. And…This is so ridiculous- I had this plan where I'd write it up, bring it to you and you were proud of me for remembering what my incident was and then we worked on it." I laughed, more out of embarrassment than humor.

"Well, for starters, it's not ridiculous!" She grabbed a dull pencil from the side of her desk. "It's a sign of wanting to see progress, although I doubt it will come to you that quickly. We're five sessions in, Alena. This is something we have to take our time with, right?"

She stayed quiet until I nodded and returned the gesture to confirm I was still sane. A small smile spreaded across her cheeks, probably out of relief.

Lynn scanned over the page one more time, placing a quick mark with the pencil on certain sentences. "I'm very proud of what you brought in. I know it's not what you were looking for but it's definitely the start of under-standing your childhood. And the best part is that it's something positive."

For once I felt a little hopeful. She was probably using cue words she learned from whatever college she went to but it was working.

"So…let's get started," Lynn opened a green notebook sitting beside her, glanced back at her copy of my prompt for the last time then turned to look at me. "Besides the fact that she triggered your memory, why did you address this assignment to your sister?"

I shrugged, "She was with me when it happened. I hate writing prompts the regular way so I pretended I was talking to her."

"Are you planning on showing this to her?"

"No. No." God, no.

"Why not?"

"I mean, I want to." My eyes shifted to my blaring red phone case, over to the door, then down to the carpet. "I have so many questions like what Dad was like with his parents and if we made pies like Mom suggested and what we did for Christmas but I feel like I'm burdening her if I ask."

Lynn's chair squeaked as she adjusted herself in her seat. That noise would be a great distraction for next time. I'll say it ruined my concentration. She'd have to bend her long toned legs to roll in a new pair of chairs. Depending on how long it takes to find them, three to ten minutes of our time together would be cut.

I heard her flip through her notebook. She sucked her teeth as she struggled to separate a page. "In our last session, you told me she wanted to talk to you about any questions you had since you told her about your diagnosis."

"Well...I know but I feel like I'm disappointing her when I don't know something."

"Has she done anything to make you feel like she's disappointed in you?"

"Yeah." I don't like how quick I was to respond to that. I looked up to see Lynn's reaction. It was the same patient stare. I felt like pulling my eyes out of their sockets. "There was this time at Uncle Benny's," I said, "She's always stoked to see him but it's so awkward for me. I have nothing in common with him. I don't even know him."

The only thing I gathered from two visits across the city was that he had huge binoculars to spy on his white neighbors only to gossip about them. He said it was better than reality TV. He called me a couple of times to tell me about something they were doing on the porch. I imagined him beer-bellied and relaxed on his couch with a half-open bag of chips at his side. I pretended I was too busy to talk.

Lynn scribbled something down. I pulled my knees to my chest, softly tapping the side of her desk with my fingertips. The air freshener in the outlet dragged out a slow hiss. Lavender and ocean breeze.

"Do you think that attempting to bond with him could jog a few memories?" she asked.

I almost laughed at the thought of it.

"Yeah, I guess." I brushed off the notion just as quickly as it came. "Delilah showed me a picture in his living room of his cat, Pico. I was told he died a few years ago. Heart disease, I think."

He was bound to kick the bucket at some point. I don't understand the grief around pets. They drool, shit, and sleep. Basically a child with extra hair. More problems, less appeal.

"Anyways," I continued, "She asked if I remembered playing with him. She kept smiling at me as if I was supposed to know but my mind went blank. Like completely blank. So, I said no. She couldn't look at me after that. I found a picture of us playing with him as a kitten in Benny's photo album. We were nine? Maybe ten? I should've felt something. Anything. She had to be disappointed in me. She didn't look back at me." I try to keep my voice stable. "I felt like I did something wrong."

The insides of my nostrils began to burn. My heart felt jumpy like when Bugs Bunny's heart beats out of his chest in cartoons. Before I'm able to stop myself, words spill out of me like vomit. "Sometimes I think Sophie feels the same way. She told me once that she thought it was weird that my family never ate dinner together. How do I respond to that? I have no idea what we did for dinner. Not a single clue."

We wade in silence for a while. A clamor of footsteps echoed from the office corridor. Car engines sputtered and zoomed across the parking lot below. I stared back at my phone case. It looked like a fuzzy red blob. I read somewhere that therapists were trained to stay quiet so you felt uncomfortable enough to keep talking. I think it had the opposite effect on me.

"It must be so difficult to carry the guilt and shame of not being able to connect with them," Lynn put down her pencil and gave me a knowing look, "If I'm hearing this right, it's making you believe they feel upset with you."

I should be more grateful that she was kind but all I could feel was a lump of resentment. She pushed a box of tissues near my hand. I took a few, rubbed them in between my fingers.

"What sucks the most is that I'll be doing so good. I'll feel like I'm making so much progress. I do the prompts. I write the affirmations. I'm great and then one fucking slip-up ruins everything." My mouth feels sticky and dry. "I can be out with Sophie and she'll be talking to me about how she's having such a great time with me while the only thing on my mind is if I'll have a slip-up where I can't remember something important to her or if I'll get triggered and have a breakdown in public."

Lynn rested her chin on her hand as she watched me. I felt like a caged animal at the zoo, head between the bars as children gave me sticky smiles. I sniffled and played with my shoelaces.

"Tell me again how they reacted when you told them about your diagnosis," she said.

I think of summer, dipping my legs in the backyard pool, chewing on a fingernail while Sophie processed the information from her hammock. I thought of Delilah, sprawled out in my bed, not looking very surprised at all.

"They were nice about it. Really understanding but talking about mood swings is different from watching me experience one."

"They're still new to understanding what your disorder is like though, right?"

"Yeah."

Lynn twirled the end of her pencil, leaving eraser flakes and white circles on the desk. "So, while you're having a hard time adjusting to your diagnosis, Delilah and Sophie are trying to understand it as well. They're going to be sad that you don't remember certain memories with them. It doesn't mean they think it's your fault."

My cheeks burned too hard to process what she was saying. I imagined the car ride home. Sophie would adjust the radio while I would wonder why my skin felt numb. It happened a lot when I was putting the pieces together after Lynn talked sense into me. I swiped my wet face hastily with the tissues. I knew she was used to seeing patients blubber and wail around her office but I couldn't help but feel uneasy about it. She leaned the tissue box towards me but I shook my head. The box went back to her side.

"I think this week you should focus more on how to be kinder to yourself." She brought up a few techniques we used last time for when I was feeling anxious. More techniques to make me love myself. "You're dealing with something that can be incredibly hard to have. You're going to make mistakes, misremember things and let out emotions in ways that you didn't think were possible. It's normal."

"It would feel normal if I didn't feel so alone."

Lynn nodded in understanding. She placed her fingertips over her mouth and furrowed her eyebrows. Right when I was about to ask what was wrong, her eyes widened slightly. "We're starting group therapy sessions in a few weeks. I don't have all of the details but I think being around other people who have similar experiences could be good for you. Only if you want to give it a shot."

She was staring directly at me with such hope in her eyes so I said yes. Sometimes I felt bad that she was trying so hard to help me.

Lynn leaned over and tapped on my copy of the letter with her nail. I didn't realize she was wearing press-ons today. They were coffee brown and white, matching her skirt. In my haze of pity, I started wondering where she bought them from.

"Give this letter to Delilah. Open up about all of the questions you have for her. Talk to Sophie about dinner too. I want you to jot down how you feel afterward." She gave me another reassuring nod. I nodded back but it was more of a tilt of the head. I was not exactly in agreement with this.

Lynn seemed satisfied with it regardless. She finished the rest of her coffee in one swig, and snatched tissues to dab her mouth. Her lipstick was still intact without a single smear.

I looked at the clock. 2:59. Our session ended in a minute. I realized I didn't want to leave.

Lynn slipped her large green bag on her shoulder, notebooks, and folders peeking out from the top. She gave me a sad smile. Not a single laugh line creased around her eyes. I blinked rapidly, folding my copy in a shaky rush before following her out the door.